THE NOODLE GAME

Written by Larry Dane Brimner • Illustrated by Christine Tripp

Children's Press®
A Division of Scholastic Inc.
New York • Toronto • London • Auckland • Sydney
Mexico City • New Delhi • Hong Kong
Danbury, Connecticut

For Kris Flynn
—L.D.B.

For my daughter Erin
—C.T.

Reading Consultants
Linda Cornwell
Coordinator of School Quality and Professional Improvement
(Indiana State Teachers Association)

Katharine A. Kane
Education Consultant
(Retired, San Diego County Office of Education and San Diego State University)

Library of Congress Cataloging-in-Publication Data

Brimner, Larry Dane.
    The noodle game / by Larry Dane Brimner; illustrated by Christine Tripp.
        p. cm. — (Rookie choices)
    Summary: Three J has the opportunity to cheat in a contest to win a new bike and
must decide what to do.
        ISBN 0-516-22157-4 (lib. bdg.)   0-516-25977-6 (pbk.) 5.95
        [1. Cheating–Fiction. 2. Contests–Fiction.] I. Tripp, Christine, ill. II. Title. III. Series.
PZ7.B767 No 2001
[E]—dc21   00-047565

This book is about **fair play**.

Gabby and Alex skidded
to a stop. Three J rattled
up beside them. They
called themselves
the Corner Kids.

"Look at that!"
Gabby said.

5

Three J read the sign
in the window.
"Win this Red Racer!
Guess how many noodles
are in the jar."

He looked at his
rusty two-wheeler.
"I sure could use
a new bike," he said.

The Corner Kids parked their bikes and dashed inside the Spinning Wheel Bike Shop. They looked at the jar.

"Phew!" said Alex.
"That's a lot of noodles."

9

Gabby was first to fill out a ticket. After writing her name, she wrote "500."

"Five hundred is a lot," she said.

Alex was next. He thought five hundred was more than a lot.

He wrote "100" on his ticket.

Three J got up close to the jar.
He counted noodles around the top.
He counted noodles up and down.

Three J picked up the jar to see how many noodles went across the bottom.

That's when he saw a square of paper taped to the jar. The number 965 was written on it.

"Guess, but don't touch,"
said Gertie from behind
the counter.

Three J put down
the jar and filled
out his ticket.

On Saturday, they returned to the bike shop to see if they had won.

On the way, Three J told Gabby and Alex about the number he saw on the jar.

21

"Is everyone ready?"
Gertie asked the crowd.
She read from a piece of paper.
"There are 965 noodles inside."

She dumped the noodles in a pile,
then said, "Katie Rogers wins
with a guess of 952."

The crowd clapped
as Katie pushed the
Red Racer out of
the store.

Gabby looked
at Three J.
"But you
knew the
right number,"
she whispered.

25

"It wouldn't have been fair," said Three J.

"I guess you're right," said Gabby.

"What number *did* you enter?" asked Alex.

Three J grinned. "Zero," he said.

They all laughed about that.

ABOUT THE AUTHOR

Larry Dane Brimner studied literature and writing at San Diego State University and taught school for twenty years. The author of more than seventy-five books for children, many of them Children's Press titles, he enjoys meeting young readers and writers when he isn't at his computer.

ABOUT THE ILLUSTRATOR

Christine Tripp lives in Ottawa, Canada, with her husband Don; four grown children—Elizabeth, Erin, Emily, and Eric; son-in-law Jason; grandsons Brandon and Kobe; four cats; and one very large, scruffy puppy named Jake.